AF368320

Elements

Myah Gibney

BookLeaf
Publishing

India | USA | UK

Elements © 2024 Myah Gibney

All rights reserved.

No part of this publication may be reproduced, stored in a retrieval system, or transmitted, in any form or by any means, electronic, mechanical, photocopying, recording or otherwise, without the prior written permission of the presenters.

Myah Gibney asserts the moral right to be identified as author of this work.

Presentation by *BookLeaf Publishing*

Web: www.bookleafpub.com

E-mail: info@bookleafpub.com

ISBN: 9789360942298

First edition 2024

To my dad, who taught me that the bits and pieces that make you up are given by those who love you...

I get all the weird pieces from you.

ACKNOWLEDGEMENT

I would like to thank my friends and coworkers for pouring over these works with me to decide which pieces deserved the title of a "human experience".

I also want to thank my friends and my family for helping me create these experiences, both positive and negative. I love you all.

PREFACE

The human experience is something that everyone has to suffer from. I wanted to offer a small snippet from my personal story of such a condition.

My poetry often comes from a place of extreme emotion, or a story that I feel needs to be told. Some of these pieces are from my earlier days of writing poetry, in college. I went through a very rough semester, and each prompt left me falling apart at the seams to tell these stories. Some weeks were too much, so I created something fictional in place of something I personally experienced. The first portion of the collection, a collection of 17 poems, contains pieces I had a part in, that I witnessed and felt and lived through. This contains snippets of my life from early childhood to today, the night that I am finishing writing all of this.

The second portion, the last 3 poems, is a set of stories that I created to show my take on the lives of others, whether through people or objects. I don't like making too many assumptions on the lives of others, but a few of these pieces are near and dear to me, and often are written out of a fervor that leaves me wondering who these stories may be about. If any of them are you, I applaud your resilience.

Some of these poems may resonate with you. Others may make no sense. Take what you need, and leave what you do not.

Tree of the Monarchy

Bent double, like old beggars under sacks,

Swinging like gnarled arms and creaking

As though ancient joints hold fast,

The limbs of the withering maple quiver.

Waiting, clinging among the orange-tipped
leaves

A cloud of fire waits. It lies, black as coal, until
a breeze

Disturbs its slumber.

Waking suddenly, exploding into existence

From seemingly thin air, heatless flames

Lick the sky, rising and fanning out

An endless expanse of orange and black

Splits apart against the clearest of blues.

Each little flame becomes its own creature

The furious flare dissipating into the day.

The Definition of Gaslighting

I tried
To be nice.

I tried to
Be civil.

I was trying my hardest
Since you can't seem to give

Up.

"These are really pretty! I promise, I won't
Let anything happen to them! I swear!"

The orange tinted one seems
So
Big, and the other seems unreal in both pink and
blue
And the watch is beautiful, and
the
maskyoumadeisreallyprettyandwhyarewetalking
aboutmemories

Dad? What does this have to do with him, why

Frozen.

As I sat on your bed, and you
        Vomited
        Word
        After
        Word
AndallIcouldthinkofwaswhatdidIdowrongwhatdi
dIdowhydidyousaythatdaddoesn'thatemewhendi
dIdo-

"All I ever did was be proud of you,
Treat you
Like an adult, why is he your favorite" And sure,
I remember those

Texts.

But you never showed up. Sure, he doesn't text
me the same things, or say it out loud, but
No matter
What I was doing, whether
Small or large, he was right

There.

I could see him.

He came to see me, in person

Every single time

And as you continue to
SPEW

IwanttoleaveIwanttogohomeIwantoutIfeelstuckI'
mintarthatclayisreallytealandIcan'tthinkofwhatIn
eedtosaywhatIhavetosay

"Did I have anything to do with that?"

Can'tmovemyhandwhyisitsoheavy
TheseareyourgrandmasdoItakethemhomeandlety
outorturemeforthembacklat-

"What did I ever do
Wrong"
"I'm having a one-sided conversation here,
aren't I"

Stand up. Stand. Up. Move. Move. Leave.
Move. Why can't I move.

They make no sound as I set them on the table,
and step to

The

Doorway over
My head.

Doorway. Gate. Open gate, open mouth.

"My daughter is a whore"
   Do you know how many times I've
repeated that in my head?
"My daughter is a whore"
   "That's a fucking lie! How dare you!"
"My daughter is a whore!"
   Mother's Day, in front of my friend's
mother
"Mydaughterisawhore"
   Do you know what that did to me?
"My daughter. Is a whore."
   "I have feelings too!"
"My. Daughter. Is. A. Whore."
   "That is a lie! I never said that!"
"I meant your sister, now shut it and stop
crying!"
   "Get out of my house!"
"If you don't quit crying, I'm taking you back to
your dad's!"

Then I shouldn't have stopped crying.
And I don't think I'll ever stop.

Writer's Block

How long had passed since she had seen
Her?
It was all she could think about. What a
cover.
It had been wood, not plastic or
cardboard.
Blue and gold, and a metal binding to
boot.
She'd only seen it once, when the drawer had
finally
opened.
As light cascaded across her purple cap, blinding
her,
A hand rummaging within the vast space,
there!
On a wood shelf behind a shoulder, on full
display,
Her.
A flash of gold as the light hit the filigree at a
delicate
angle,
Seemingly riding the curves and soft flicks of
the
design.
And as quickly as the drawer had been opened,

darkness.
Her nights and days filled with rolling about,
trying
So hard to get the attention of someone,
anyone.
But as she tried so hard to remember that
beautiful
cover,
As she knocked and knocked against that dark
barrier,
No one came.

Mirrors, Mirrors, and Mirrors

Bodies constantly judged
Harshly, large or small
"You must be starving yourself"
"Quit eating, you've had enough"
Passing in the hallway, bowed heads and
Hurried whispers, giggles echoing behind
Nasty, poison-dripped words
Jabbing in turned backs.
Called prude and ugly for wearing something
Long?
Called slutty and a whore for trying to stay
Cool.

Have you ever been just trying to get home to
your dorm after a long day
And heard someone yell at you from a window
high in the sky
"Hey! You're a fat fuck!"
And you refuse to look up, to even acknowledge
you've heard a word as you
shove
Your earbuds further in?
That night, you look at yourself sideways
in the mirror,
in a bra and shorts
And you can't look at yourself again for the next
two weeks.

Thank You

You lifted it.
That weight
You lifted it away.
With three words, you took away the feeling I'd
been dragging with me

Like
a
ball
and
chain.....

It melted away down my face as you said it.
It broke a barrier in my brain as I heard it.
I broke into pieces and formed something new
as I processed it.

I thought that I was crazy.
It told me I was crazy.
That growl-y little crazy
voice that took away my sanity.

I thought maybe it was right.
I made it up right
on the spot, that the right

story was what I'd gotten wrong.

"I was there."

...You were?

"I was there. I remember. You didn't make it up."

I became a puddle in your arms, a sobbing
puddle
hunched over from carrying the thought that I
was evil.

You made me light again.

History Doesn't Repeat Itself..

Why did I unblock your phone number?

He asked me to call you.

Why do I go along like nothing happened?

Because if I don't, you'll just whine and cry and act like you're the one under a fist.

Why do I treat this like it's ok?

Because it's the only thing I know how to do.

Why do I feel bad if I hear you crying?

Because until six years ago, I didn't think you were the problem. I'm still learning where it truly lies.

Why do I let you interrupt my happiness?

....I don't know.

Why do I let you ruin every single little thing
and answer when it's convenient for you?

I don't know.

....Why are you still part of my life?

I don't... know.

But It Often Rhymes

I don't... know.

....Why are you still part of my life?

I don't know.

Why do I let you ruin every single little thing
and answer when it's convenient for you?

....I don't know.

Why do I let you interrupt my happiness?

Because until six years ago, I didn't think you
were the problem. I'm still learning where it
truly lies.

Why do I feel bad if I hear you crying?

Because it's the only thing I know how to do.

Why do I treat this like it's ok?

Because if I don't, you'll just whine and cry and
act like you're the one under a fist.

Why do I go along like nothing happened?

He asked me to call you.

Why did I unblock your phone number?

Identity

A poem starting on the right is a bit jarring

Compared to one started on the left,

Or in the middle.

I feel like a poem on the right.
I feel like sharing something abnormal.
Something weird I may say, or something I do.

I can eat an entire can of salt and vinegar
pringles in one go.
It may burn my tongue until the next morning,
but I'll do it.

I once jokingly called myself a whore (very
loudly)
in a bagel shop to my new roommate and
made my friend nearly choke on her drink.

No. I won't give you context for what I say, but
I'll gladly share more.

I like being a poem on the right.

I like laughing about one friend's shortness in
                          one breath and whining,
    of course not seriously, when they call me
                          "granny" in the next.

We'll shout "fuck you" at each other across the
                          dish room while working,
    and make our boss concerned when we talk
                          about a 3-month timer
                          before anyone can die.

I learned how to sign "power bottom" just to
                          mess with a friend,
    and taught it to the rest of the group to tease
                          him.

                    I love being a poem on the right!

I can spew about the most recent seven book
                          series I've been reading

    when I hit a plot twist, and my friends will
                          listen,
    letting me word vomit my happy little
                          hyper-focused heart out.

                    We can talk until three am

about the fact that someone with dyslexia might
read
"Bilbo Baggins" as "Dildo Daggins".
Why we got on that topic, I have no clue.
But it's just as funny without knowing why.

I can share insanely random fun facts I found out
of nowhere that might
pertain to the conversation, or might totally
derail from it.

Like the fact that dolphins get high by tossing
pufferfish around with their noses.

Did you know that the reason Lord Farquaad is
called Lord Farquaad is
because it sounds like fu-

Oh, yeah, and humans have stripes.

Like, skin pattern. It's just invisible to us.
But cats can see it. So, cats see us with stripes.
Weird, right?

But being a poem on the right is hard.

Being a poem on the right only works when
people want to

read the poem in a way that might be
uncomfortable.

Sometimes, I'm forced to be

A poem in the middle.

When my family gets confused about my latest
obsession, I force myself into their
conversation, only really talking when I find it
actually interesting.

Yeah, sure, I like Huskers football.
Oh, yeah, the bees are really active this time of
year.

Oh, that reminds me!
Did you know that we as humans have stripes on
our skin?

Oh. You don't...
really seem to care. Ok.

Yeah, the river is really low. The downed trees
on the sandbars look super cool!

And now they're talking about some random
family member

I've met maybe twice having issues with their
land.
Wow.
That sure does suck for them, huh?

And then...
I just stay silent,
in my corner,
playing on my phone,
missing being on the right again.

I may have fun writing on the left, or in the
middle. That's ok.

But being stuck on the left for others' comfort
and readability feels
wrong.

Give me the oddball any day. Let me be weird.
Because

Reading a poem from the right disrupts your
head,
even for a second.

And I love it.

The Lair of the Beast

Jaws wide enough to swallow an elephant in one
snap
Darker than the night, waiting, prowling in the
black
It lurks, its presence looming as a jagged
mountain
Every time it shuts its maw, I struggle between
the teeth
Cutting myself open on the serrated edges until
free.

It slithers back into its dank home, constantly
looming
Breathing down my neck
Until pouncing, it drags me into the dark with it,
restarting
The entire affair again.
Its claws take hold, gouging out stone and
sending sparks
Into the air, igniting
Sending shocks of hot, searing pain through me.

My pain is the blackest dragon in the deepest
cave,
Swallowing me down and cutting old scars open
again.
With every loss, he leaps
Chewing on my heart like a toy.
Turning my brain into a personal scratching
post.
I am at his mercy.

The Final Resting Place

The thrill of the final blackout, as the audience
lets loose a thunderstorm in the enclosed
space.
Each roar as the seconds spin around, chest
dancing to a silent song only it can hear.
Lights up, cheering, and bowing to the faces of
those who'd watched with the attention
of vultures,
Singing as we head out for the final time
amongst the lights swimming in the concrete
rivers
and carpet boulders.

I feel the pin pricks at the corner of my eyes, but
the cheers echoing through the hall
make it bearable.
The sequins on everyone turn into constellations
in a bright, sunlit orange hallway
Everything runs, moving so fast I can't tell that
an hour has flown over us, wings wide
and silent.
As the silver starry mist that used to decorate our
heads settles into the black, empty space, I

get gathered into arms that I've come to know,
pressed to chests and given declarations,
promises that this isn't my last.

Not yet.

Promises that we have one last one together, one
more time.

I will see you again.

I will see you, here, once more, to create
something visceral.

We will walk again with the ghosts that fill this
place, some long forgotten, and some
now striding within for the first time:

An ancient, cranky old lady from a forgotten
civilization laughs, wheezing as she jokes with a
flush faced, freezing ship captain.

A villager with no name dances with her child
and her husband, inviting a very reluctant,
prude puritan judge to join them.

Flashing her jewelry in the blinking, Vegas
lights, a woman blinded by fame recalls tales of
her
freak-show and life to that of a flamboyant,
poetic Italian man, everything up to how she met
her husband.

A hulking, slightly oblivious German man
laments his woes of no money and strange men
to a talking bird from the jungles of India, and a
very tired school counselor.

They are not gone. They may be forgotten by
most, but they will never leave.

For they are home.

Seat C, Aisle 24

I wanted an aisle seat
The first time I took a plane somewhere

I was terrified.

We were seated   side by side
High school kids   most of us
Going into the   world for the
Very first time   across the country
In some metal   contraption meant to
Ferry us above   where we had
Lived most of   our short lives

The rumble of the engines made my heart nearly
bust from my chest
The invisible hand pushing me back into my seat
as the plane gathered its speed

The hand clasped in mine as we waited, for the
first time
To find ourselves where humans were NOT
supposed to be.
I peeked over my friend's shoulder, wanting to
see for just a moment

The buildings turning to dots and the fields
turning to tiles and-

My stomach turned, forcing me to grab my book
and read it, shoving my earbuds further in.

The second time wasn't so bad, on the way
home. I sat closer to the window, then.
My heart thundered, but less so out of fear.

I wouldn't take a plane again for 5 years. But I
would, and I would go alone.
I was texting my father, and my best friend
updates. But I was alone.

I boarded
                              alone,
and waited for it to take off
                              alone.

This time, my heart was pounding from
something other than fear.

Because of this weird, insane, death defying
machine..

I could go far away.

I could explore.
I can see friends, have new experiences, and be
free.

As I walked down the aisle, I decided to choose
something different. So...

I watch out the window, to see the quilted
landscape, and the pillowed clouds, and the rest
of the world from a distance.

Anytime I take a plane somewhere
I want the window seat.

Why Do You Care?

I don't care what anyone thinks.

I'm not hurting anyone.

I don't care what they think.

It's not wrong.

I don't care what you think.

I'm an adult.

I don't care. What you think.

It's nerdy, so what?

I. Do. Not. Care. What. You. Think.

It's kinda weird, but I'm happy.

I DON'T CARE WHAT YOU THINK!

I don't even know why you care.

I don't care what you think!

I know it's not "normal"…

I don't care what you think.

I know I'll get upset when you make a joke..

But I don't care what you think…

I'll forget when I'm laughing.

But I'll care what you think…

If you comment on my photos.

Because I'll care what you think.

If I share what I'm doing

Because I'm worried about what you think.

In that I think about what you say

Because I'm scared of what you think.

Dual-Purpose

There is some sick duality in what happened that day.

The night before I was supposed to go in

The night before I was supposed to be free

The night that we found out

The night that we learned about

The night you became labeled with it

The night you became a statistic for

The night I came to terms with

The night I came to wish for

The next day, we both were in the hospital

I went in to have them removed

I went in to have myself changed

You were there under watchful eye

You were there under careful hands

I came out feeling happy, guilty

I came out feeling nauseous, strong

You stayed in looking scared, downtrodden

You stayed in looking weak, defeated

I came to see you, shuffling like a zombie

You sat in that bed, I sat in the window

You sat in that bed, we talked about me

I left a bit later, watching out the window

I left a bit later, and something in me broke

There was some perverse mind at work.

33

Love Language

Everyone shows love in different ways.

Some show it through their actions.

The most loving of hugs, the kindest of caresses,

A helping hand and a blanket handed off when
you're silently shivering.

Some show it through their thoughts.

Photos sent to you with a simple "This reminds
me of you"

Video links that are connected to the things
you've blabbered about.

But the love you've shown me is around me at
all times.

The soft collection of plushies that I've
accumulated from you over the years.

A keychain, a small trinket, something I can
hold in my hands.

The goofiest little magnets that I giggle at.

As I sit here, the newest member of my
collection stares at me,

Peeking out from their little box.

You show your love by letting me rant far into
the night, giving me space to share

My own goofy form of love.

You sit with me when I have no ability to
function, and let me work through it by

Just being there.

You have been there for so long.

Your love pervades every corner of my life,
through the good and the bad.

It is the type of love I'd never change.

The Process of Being A Sister

I cannot speak to those of a singular nature

Who have not had the experience of an upper or lower hand.

I cannot speak to those who did not have to sit on the couch

While someone shoves their bare feet up your shirt.

I cannot speak to those who did not participate in evening shouting matches

Over the jar of pickle juice in the fridge that you both wanted.

I cannot speak to those who did not form the best connection

With someone who was just a bit further in age from you.

I cannot speak to those who did not argue over the dumbest

Of topics, those which have been lost to time.

I cannot speak to those who haven't experienced

Life's most interesting relationship.

However....

I can speak to those who have experienced late nights spent giggling together

Watching TV when you're supposed to be asleep.

I can speak to those who have experienced a re-connection later in life,

Learning you have so much more in common.

I can speak to those who have shared memories galore,

In the same bedroom for years at a time.

I can speak to those who have broken down crying, knowing exactly who

You're going to call to help you get through it.

I can speak to those who had been snuck a little
alcohol before a wedding

In a camper, before they were of age.

I can speak to those who experienced watching
someone grow up

And helping them in their own track to life.

I can speak to those who found a friend,

Within the walls of their own home.

Patchwork

It's fuzzy.

Things are fuzzy.

I'm missing these little pieces.

You tell me that this happened, and I think it did.

But I don't remember. It seems...Wrong.

Why am I missing little bits of my life?

What did you do?

What happened to me?

Why have parts of me faded into the darkness?

Trying to replace them is like shoving something
vaguely shaped right into the wrong hole,
pasting it over with glue, and waiting for it to
magically fit.

I can't keep doing this. I can't patch myself up
like a quilt.

How do I fix this?

The Art of Love; A Study in Statues

Loving you is loving something I cannot touch.

Loving you is loving something about the littlest things.

Why does loving you make every part of me hurt?

Why does loving you make my head spin like a top?

Loving you is loving something about the little things.

Loving you is loving the little pieces you've given me.

Why do I find myself looking at everything I do and seeing you?

Why do I find myself waiting to hear from you
at any minute, any day?

Loving you is loving the little pieces you've
given me.

Loving you is being crushed by the biggest
pieces into dust.

Why does loving you make me feel so guilty?

Why does loving you have to make me feel like
a bad person?

Loving you is being crushed by those big pieces
into dust.

Loving you is loving something I cannot touch.

Back and Forth... Back and Forth...

How is it possible to get this amount of joy

Out of something as simple as sitting on the couch for 2 hours to watch a show together?

How is it possible to get this amount of love

Out of something as simple as talking on the phone for 5 minutes?

How is it possible to gain enough serotonin

From watching a daily count showing that you've kept in contact with someone every day for almost 3 years straight?

How is it possible to feel this much love

And yet... Some days it still feels like it's drained away from your life?

How is it possible to feel this alone

When you've got people caring when you drop
off the face of the Earth?

How is it possible to feel like it can drift away

Like a boat on the horizon?

Why is love so inconsistent?

A Sailor's Guardian

She watches from the cliff
Waiting for her love to return from the sea.

She watches from the cliff
Under the growing hawthorn tree.

She watches from the cliff
The lighthouse burning brightly.

She watches from the cliff
White hair, but despite, sprightly.

She watches from the cliff
As 30 years have passed.

She watches from the cliff
Her lovers ship on the waves, outcast.

She watches from the cliff
The hawthorn tree above.

She watches from the cliff
A bird cries in the sky above.

She watches from the cliff

The branches surround her now.

She watches from the cliff
His embrace remaining in the boughs.

Cigarettes

She held out her hand for a cigarette.

The hand that held mine, hoisting me up after
falling on my ass
Because I'd been slammed in the face with a
cartoon sounding rubber ball.

The hand that had slipped me note after note,
and had met my face
When I daydreamed of her face in mine, waving
me to reality.

The hand that grabbed mine as we ran down the
hallways
Laughing while the bitch who'd bullied me cried
out, the condoms in her locker falling to the
floor.

The hand slipping me extra food, when she
found out Mom lost her job,
So she stole some from her own pantry.

The hand that knocked on my window, dragged
me out the frame and taught me the
Best places in town to stargaze.

The hand that helped me zip up my graduation
gown, and smooth the frizzed bits of my braid,
minutes before being the cause of its undoing.

The hand that touched me, my life, every little
bit of me, until I knew it better than myself,
Holding a velvet box and a blue-gemmed ring.

The hand that held mine as we promised to each
other, that we
Would never let go, that everything was what we
wanted.

The hand that gripped mine as we waited for the
results,
Squeezed tighter with each failed implant.

The hand that accidentally slapped the doctor in
her excitement
When the first embryo took.

The hand that touched our son's face, as he slept
in my arms,
Traced every feature and committed it to
memory.

The hand that slammed shut the door when we
discovered he

Wouldn't make it past one.

The hand that broke picture after picture against
the wall
On the day she missed his last breath.

The hand that wandered, found comfort in
others, and left
My side for someone else.

The hand that offered me those papers, that
Once touched me gently, avoiding every graze.

The hand that opened the door, and signed that
dotted line
Committing every promise to a grave beside our
boy.

She held out her hand for a cigarette.

Burnout

I wake to the sound of a crackling match
The gaze of bright sun fading to black
He writes with fervor, frantic, that wretch.
As page after page drops, ripped, crumpled, that
stack
My back begins to hunch, but the pile grows, his
face framed in light
Frustration, anger, wonder, and allure
Pen nibs, broken, tossed in and forgotten
Flickering light, time is fading. Do I see failure?
His hands shake, like they have been frostbitten.

The sound of scratches in the air, as pen
Meets parchment, desperate in the search for
Something long gone, a thought that again
Breezes his mind, but the dark seeps indoors.

All I see is his face, features melding in the dark
As I fall asleep, one final page falling to the
murk.

www.ingramcontent.com/pod-product-compliance
Lightning Source LLC
La Vergne TN
LVHW050936200726
843508LV00011B/2360